Jj

Kelly Doudna

ABDO
Publishing Company

Published by SandCastle™, an imprint of ABDO Publishing Company, 8000 West 78th Street, Edina, Minnesota 55439.

Printed in the United States of America, North Mankato, Minnesota.

012000 022013

Cover and interior photo credits: Artville, Comstock, Eyewire Images, PhotoDisc

Library of Congress Cataloging-in-Publication Data

Doudna, Kelly, 1963-
    Jj / Kelly Doudna.
      p. cm. -- (The alphabet)
    Includes index.
    ISBN 1-57765-403-X (hardcover)
    ISBN 1-59197-010-5 (paperback)
    1. Readers (Primary) [1. Alphabet.] I. Title.

PE1119 .D6759 2000
428.1--dc21
[[E]]
                                                              00-028883

The SandCastle concept, content, and reading method have been reviewed and approved by a national advisory board including literacy specialists, librarians, elementary school teachers, early childhood education professionals, and parents.

Let Us Know

After reading the book, SandCastle would like you to tell us your stories about reading. What is your favorite page? Was there something hard that you needed help with? Share the ups and downs of learning to read. We want to hear from you! To get posted on the Abdo Publishing Company Web site, send us email at:

sandcastle@abdopub.com

About SandCastle™

A professional team of educators, reading specialists, and content developers created the SandCastle™ series to support young readers as they develop reading skills and strategies and increase their general knowledge. The SandCastle™ series has four levels that correspond to early literacy development in young children. The levels are provided to help teachers and parents select the appropriate books for young readers.

Emerging Readers
(no flags)

Beginning Readers
(1 flag)

Transitional Readers
(2 flags)

Fluent Readers
(3 flags)

These levels are meant only as a guide. All levels are subject to change.

To see a complete list of SandCastle™ books and other nonfiction titles from ABDO Publishing Company, visit **www.abdopublishing.com** or contact us at:
8000 West 78th Street, Edina, Minnesota 55439 • 1-800-800-1312 • fax: 1-952-831-1632

We join Jay for fun.

Jill jumps rope.

Jill and Jacki jump together.

Jenna jumps over Julie.

Jenny wears a pink jumper.

Jeff and Jim color.

Jon helps with the jack-o-lantern.

Jane enjoys her juice.

What does June wear?

(jacket)

Words I Can Read

Nouns

A noun is a person, place, or thing

fun (FUHN) p. 5
jacket (JAK-it) p. 21
jack-o-lantern (JAK-uh-lan-turn) p. 17
juice (JOOSS) p. 19
jumper (JUHM-pur) p. 13
rope (ROHP) p. 7

Proper Nouns

A proper noun is the name
of a person, place, or thing

Jacki (JAK-ee) p. 9
Jane (JAYN) p. 19
Jay (JAY) p. 5
Jeff (JEF) p. 15
Jenna (JEN-uh) p. 11

22

Verbs

A verb is an action or being word

More Jj Words

jar

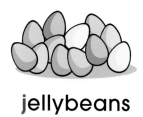

jellybeans

jet

jungle